Other titles in the UWAP Poetry series (established 2016)

Anh &
Lucien

Tony Page

For three decades, Tony was a teacher in Australia and Asia, mainly in the fields of Literature, History and Drama. His last position was as Head of Performing Arts at an international school in Bangkok, where he mounted numerous stage productions, from Shakespeare and Sophocles to agitprop and modern dance. Tony is the author of six poetry collections: *They're Knocking at my Door*, 1988; *Satellite Link*, 1992; *Gateway to the Sphinx*, 2004; *Who Killed Caravaggio?*, 2015; *Dawn the Proof*, 2016 and *Back to Earth*, 2019. He has been active in the Australian poetry scene since the 1980s, as well as reading from his work at the Edinburgh Festival, in Venice, Paris, and at various venues in the US.

Tony Page
Anh &
Lucien

UW A P Poetry

First published in 2020 by
UWA Publishing
Crawley, Western Australia 6009
www.uwap.uwa.edu.au

UWAP is an imprint of UWA Publishing,
a division of The University of Western Australia.

THE UNIVERSITY OF
WESTERN
AUSTRALIA

Copyright © Tony Page 2020
The moral right of the author has been asserted.
ISBN 978-1-76080-146-5

A catalogue record for this
book is available from the
National Library of Australia

Designed by Becky Chilcott, Chil3
Typeset in Lyon Text by Lasertype
Printed by McPherson's Printing Group

 uwapublishing

MIX
Paper from
responsible sources
FSC
www.fsc.org FSC® C001695

Contents

Only connect the prose and the passion, and both will be exalted.
E.M. Forster

It is the fight between tiger and elephant.
Ho Chi Minh

Chronology of Events

1901

Lucien d'Accroché born, Toulon, France.

1918

Trinh Anh Duy born, Hanoi, French Indochina.

1925

December: Phan Boi Chau, pioneer of 20th century Vietnamese nationalism, released into house arrest. Anh accompanies his father to the trial.

1940

March: Anh arrested in Paris for participating in a student demonstration. Stripped of his scholarship, he is sent back to Hanoi

April: Lucien arrested for 'public indecency'. To avoid a scandal, his brother arranges to have him join the Foreign Service in Indochina.

June: France defeated by Germany, which rules approximately two-thirds of the country. The remaining part of France, and the French colonies, under a nominally independent government, headed by Marshal Pétain, with its capital at Vichy.

September: The Vichy Government signs a treaty, allowing the Imperial Japanese Armed Forces use of all its military bases in Indochina

October: Pétain and Hitler 'share a cordial meeting', Montoire-sur-le-Loire, France

December: Anh and Lucien meet on the steps of the Hanoi Opera House.

1941

February: Ho Chi Minh returns to Vietnam and establishes his base in a cave at Pac Bo in Cao Bằng Province, near the Sino-Vietnamese border.

May: Formation of 'The League for the Independence of Vietnam', usually known as 'The Viet Minh'.

1944

December: Lucien arrested for 'collaborating with the enemy' by French police. Anh escapes and joins Ho Chi Minh's guerrilla forces.

1945

May: Lucien executed, *Maison Centrale*, Hanoi's political prison.

August: Viet Minh troops enter Hanoi.

September: Ho Chi Minh declares Vietnamese independence. Anh learns of Lucien's execution and visits the condemned man's cell, *Maison Centrale*.

Anh remembers the trial of Phan Boi Chau

I can't forget the day my father took me to see Phan Boi Chau: Confucian master, national hero, minor god. It was 1925 and I was only seven. Would we be among the first Vietnamese to observe the French High Criminal Commission in action? There he was at last. A bald gentleman with wispy beard in traditional dress, looking nothing like the famed political activist I'd heard about. Was this the legendary champion who'd campaigned so long for Indochina's independence? He looked just like any other old man. But when my father held me high, I could see how Phan stared into the four judges' faces, one by one. Fifteen years of prison hadn't destroyed him. *Remember this courtroom, my boy,* my father whispered. *Never forget what you're seeing here today: the beginning of your country's freedom.*

Anh returns to Hanoi after two years' study in France

This morning about to dock at Haiphong Harbour, fifteen years after that pivotal day, his words echo through my body again, though everything's been turned upside down since then. I now oppose everything my father stands for, but have to admit it was because of Phan's trial that I discovered Marxism and joined the revolutionary movement. Of course, I can't reveal any of this to *Cha*. He's outraged I lost the scholarship in Paris and may disown me if he learnt the real reason for my expulsion. He was already angry two years ago about something else. Must remain clear-headed when he probes me for details, as he surely will. How long before he taunts me again for not being the son he dreamt would follow in his steps?

Lucien sails to Hanoi leaving his homeland

What do I care if they send me into exile? Hitler's bullies are swooping down on France. It is far better to be out of the way, on the edge of our mock heroic empire. Who knows, if it is anything like the Orient of my fantasies, I may never want to return. All those white uniforms, the starched bureaucracy, the military marionettes, pale skins strutting through jungles. The whole enterprise smacks so much of theatre, I am sure to find a role for a few years, perhaps even a lifetime. If we can only manage to keep the operetta rolling on, if the farce proves to have some kind of substance beneath its exotic allure.

In the Indian Ocean Lucien reveals deeper motives

I have been edging this way for years. It was the Colonial Exhibition in Paris which set me on my journey; those dioramas of vines strangling themselves, the papier-mâché models of temples in ruin, the costumes with their libidinous silks. Then the School of the Far East and all those months in the silence of its library, poring over the diaries of our nineteenth century explorers. Eventually, I had traced every journey, copying each faded map in my own hand. Next, I found an agent from whom I began buying smuggled artefacts: Champa statues snapped at the neck, diaphanous winged spirit-messengers and Khmer inscriptions which I struggled to decipher. But above all, the sandstone carving here in my hand – fourteenth century Angkor style – the face of a god with his baffling smile. It is this talisman which draws me now across the seas.

Anh descends the gangplank into another world

Porters scramble for position, vendors frantically arrange their wares, swarms of hucksters jostle the passengers in front of me. I'm shocked to admit the smell is revolting, the noise and shoving overwhelming. So, these are my fellow countrymen, the oppressed I'm meant to be fighting for? Far easier to love them in the abstract, on the other side of the world, where they were text book examples of the proletariat. This revulsion won't last, will it? It's only because I've been living in what now seems another world. Just wait a few days and I'm sure to feel solidarity with my Annamese brothers once more. In the meantime, must be careful not to let it show. Confronting *Cha* will be crisis enough for one day. All those sarcastic comments about my manhood. Why I was glad to get away in the first place.

Lucien enters his residence in the Diplomatic Corps

The officer assigned me introduces *les domestiques*, dolls in uniforms with finely chiselled features. Will I ever become accustomed to servants as fiercely neat as these Annamese? Then we enter the cavernous kitchen where an indeterminate number of natives are cooking unfamiliar foods. Each time I turn or take a step, they begin a series of deep bows, rippling around the walls like a wave. My officer is eager to finish these duties and join his fellow civil servants for a high time on the town. He smiles with barely concealed relief as he wishes me good night. I also am pleased to see him leave. Such posturing fatigues me at the best of times, more so now that I am overwhelmed by the heat. Ever since the ship berthed in Hanoi, my brain has been inundated by so many logic-defying sights and smells that I fear I will drown.

Lucien shudders in his new sleeping quarters

I hope these curtains are heavy enough to block out the heat. As my eyes adjust, it is clear there is not one Asian object in the entire room, all the furniture defiantly European. The wallpaper with its oak trees and autumn leaves reminds me how far I am from 'home'. Their foliage shudders with the memory of that escapade in the back streets of Toulon, the reason I have been exiled here. My 'honourable appointment' to the Diplomatic Corps, what a mockery! Surely some of them know. That explains why the officer did not invite me to accompany him. The hypocrisy! They certainly smell it, while being masters at pretending not to notice. Perhaps they are laughing over a drink right now? But that night in Toulon was no joke.

Anh looks in the mirror

At last, my brothers have gone out and I have the bedroom to myself. Let's check in the mirror and see if my muscles slackened on the boat. Still look OK, so all that work under Heng Tu paid off. When I met him five years ago, he started training me in martial arts. That's why my chest and stomach are so firm. Let's see how high I can kick. About the same as before. Wish Heng could see that, he'd be proud. If it weren't for him, I'd still be nothing but a skinny rake, stuck to my desk. It's only because of Heng I've grown strong enough to make a good soldier when the time comes to fight. Bac Ho will be pleased with this machine I've prepared for the revolution.

Memories sink beneath the skin

Look at the array of cleaning agents in my new bathroom, meticulously arranged by the servants. But can any of them wash off the misery of the shanty towns I was driven through to reach this place? Even less possible to cleanse myself of the stain from that night in Toulon. The police certainly enjoyed themselves softening me up before interrogation. If they are like that with one of their own, God knows what they must do to the poor natives here. It was only because Gabriel, my brother the colonel, made them aware of the scandal which would occur if they proceeded to court, that they let me go at all. Then the spider's web he had to weave to get me posted here as a way of sweeping dust under the carpet. Do they expect me to have a less hypocritical conscience than their own? I will play their game and keep appearances *clean*.

Lucien unpacks books in his new study

The Greek philosophers and a few volumes of Voltaire, what an odd combination, alongside such works as the history of Buddhism and Angkor temple style, yet all seem to have weathered the ocean voyage. *Papa* wanted me to read to him in his final days, sitting by the bedside as my brother and his children came to take their farewell. A benediction, however, he would not bestow on me. *Maman* refused to be consoled when he died, as she did when learning the reason for my arrest. Although shocked by the scandal, she did not want me to leave. Now then, let me try to sleep in this wretched climate, wondering if I will ever see her again.

Lucien wakes to the first morning in a new zone

The heat squeezes my lungs. Breathing requires conscious effort. The sheets, a battlefield of perspiration. This incessant noise, the subterranean hum of Asia. Endless hammering, shouting, weaving. As if life needs susurration simply to maintain itself. The world leaps through my bedroom like a tiger. Stumbling to the window, I struggle with the latch. Does everything rust in this climate? Blinking against what threatens to be sunlight without pity, I take a gulp of whisky and totter into the first full day of exile.

Anh's first foray into Hanoi since his return

I'm out the door before *Cha* comes downstairs. Away from his scolding about the scholarship and what he calls 'that shamefulness' with Heng Tu. Outside, that's better – I'd forgotten how crowded the streets are. Much easier riding a bicycle here than in Paris, almost no cars to worry about. I merge into the silent throng of cyclists as if I'd never left. Look at all those wheels seeming to float above the road, gliding without touching, like schools of fish. I'll visit the Old Quarter and see if each of the twisting lanes still houses its specialised trade. Yep, Hang Bo churns out handwoven baskets, Hang Da produces leather goods, Hang Non displays its fanfare of hats. How strange to hear Annamese spoken again; its tones strike my eardrums like fists. Odd, no one's staring at me. I'm no longer the foreigner, as I was made to feel every day in France. No one even gives me a second glance. What a relief. Don't need to be on guard against a hostile world.

Lucien unearths some secrets in the Diplomatic Corps

It did not take long to find a place where I can hide. I have arranged a table and chair in the corner, badly lit but often refreshingly cool. Most of the time, I am assured of solitude. No one asks what files I read with increasing fascination and disgust. Each week, I plough through another stack. It is almost comical how the police prefer to arrest suspects under cover of darkness. As if they revel in the clandestine nature of their work against local groups fighting for independence. I try to picture the interrogations. How long does it take for the blood to dry? What are the procedures if someone dies during torture? When imagination fails me, I look out the window at the trees spooling long shadows against the Ministry buildings, the shutters opening on to stately balconies taking in the brief respite of sunset. How neat of the French, bringing such style to our colonies.

Lucien's carving begins to surface in strange places

I take the carving from my pocket, stroking it in a ritual which has become almost an obsession. The sandstone warrior – pillaged from some temple wall – in a perpetual dream, his eyes half-closed while raising a sword, more like a dance than any battle pose. It was his smile which unnerved me at first sight years ago, his frozen serenity pursuing me ever since. Unexpectedly the smile appears in a mirror at the Residence, in a Ministry police record, or simply passing by in the street.

Anh makes contact with the local revolution

They're suspicious and make me wait a long time. Finally, they find the comrade who knows about my French Party membership and the campaigns I joined at University. At first, he's angry because I was arrested during a demonstration on the steps of *L'Assemblé Nationale*, saying it gave the Party bad publicity. I begin trying to defend myself, but he silences me with a sweep of the hand, almost like *Cha*. Obviously, this was only a test, because now he smiles: *You showed considerable courage for someone your age.* He invites two other cadres to join us and closes the door, saying: *Well done, Comrade. Let's talk about what you can do for us now you're back in Hanoi.*

Anh cannot sleep

They must think I'm completely useless! The Party refuses to let me join Bac Ho and his guerrillas in the mountains. They claim I'm more useful teaching factory workers in the Mass Literacy Campaign. What an insult – just because I used to be a good student! I've dreamt of nothing else for months, fighting to free my people. I long to be out there, ranging in those provinces on the maps in Party HQ. Only an hour ago, I was listening to comrades who had returned from the jungle, with all their tales of adventure. Can't possibly sleep because I hear the leaves rustling and the animals crawling in the undergrowth, as my unit moves towards the battle lines. I will force them to let me fight.

Attitudes towards homosexuality in Vietnam

A Compendium of Universal Sexuality: *Historically, there has been relatively little mention of male sexuality in Vietnam, although some emperors of the sixteenth and seventeenth centuries are said to have maintained male concubines. The Vietnamese use more than one expression for the Western neologism 'homosexuality', but all have the same underlying meaning of 'half man and half woman'. For example,* Dong Tinh Luyen Ai *is a literal translation via Chinese of 'homosexuality', which dates back to 1869. This term appeared in a French-Vietnamese Dictionary of 1936, and therefore may have had some currency in the journalistic vocabulary of the 1930s. Nevertheless, the concept of 'homosexuality' will not enter general parlance until the introduction of Western sexology, so-called 'hygiene manuals' of the 1950s.* Ai Nam Ai Nu *is the closest approximation to what is meant by the Western term 'homosexuality', even though it can also refer to 'bisexual' behaviour. It did not come into use until the end of the 1930s.*

Anh imagines his plight as a fable

One fine morning in the province of Trinh, after grazing in the forest, a fawn named Ai Nam Ai Nu went with the other young deer to drink in a stream. He did not care to look at his reflection in the water, because it seemed he was not growing the same way as the others. He had heard them whispering several times before as they approached the bank, but they would stop suddenly when he tried to join them. Today, however, they began laughing at him quite openly, so that he was ashamed and slipped back into the shadows.

Anh writes to Ho Chi Minh who is hiding in the jungle

Esteemed Bac Ho, Please allow me to address you like this, even though we've never met. I've admired you for years. You're so brave, struggling for liberation from our imperialist oppressors. (Is that still the correct term? It's what I learnt in Paris, but perhaps you've thought of an expression more suited to our nationalist cause?) You've given up any chance of a personal life, sacrificing yourself for the masses. I try to imagine what your daily routine must be like. They say you're really fit, so I picture you practising martial arts by the campfire before sunrise. Do you visualise the enemy while kicking and punching among the trees? Let me prove how pure my heart is for the cause. *Respectfully your student, Trinh Anh Duy.*

Lucien copes with the solitude of his new life

Everyone has left by the time I finish with another batch of files. It is the usual crowd at *La Plantation*, where the foreign bachelors gather each evening. Some look my way and exchange whispers before resuming their meal. I am used to it now. The first few weeks, I attempted to fit in: joining the tennis club, meeting the wives of colleagues who mounted matchmaking plans which suddenly evaporated. Most nights, I end up in a bar where nobody cares how many spirits I consume. There are whole days when I speak to no one except in the office. That is why I begin to explore the back lanes of the Old Quarter, each week venturing further from the Administration's perfectly planned grid.

Lucien writes to his mother in Vichy France

Chère Maman, I trust you have received the telegram I sent upon arrival in Hanoi, so you would no longer fret about my safety. That was five days ago, but already it seems much longer. Even though shocked by my arrest, you did not want me sent to the other side of the world. It must be difficult living alone in that big house. I miss you also. Have you been out in the garden, as you promised? This month is such a beautiful time of year, it would be a pity to stay indoors. Make sure you get out for a walk each day. Have you heard from Gabriel? I am informed his regiment is preparing to move in the next few days. It is difficult to be more precise, as so much is now deemed classified, even for me. I realise nothing I say will stop you from worrying on his account but try not to let your anxiety become debilitating, as it has in the past. We have discussed this many times. Maman, please keep the promise you made. *Ton fils, Lucien.*

Recruitment Posters for the French Colonial Service

Just as Rome civilised the barbarians beyond its borders, we too have a duty to extend French culture to the backward peoples of the world/Expert Men and Technicians, the Empire entreats You!/ To uphold our traditions, enlist in the *Xth Infantry battalion*. French Republic, Ministry of War/Daring Parachutists: This is our Chance, our Realm, our Glory, our Conflict/Subscribe to the National Loan and Victory is ours!/Indochina beseeches the Empire, rally to its defence. Frenchmen, commit yourselves!/Our Colonial Troops invite you to take an exotic journey/Enrol in the National Association for Indochina *(subscription 10 Francs)*, to ensure we are delivered from the enemy and prosper in peace/Three Colours *(European, African, Asian)* all united by One Flag, One Empire/You are a Man. Go to Indochina and defend Liberty. You will become a True Leader!

Anh pleads with Uncle Ho to intervene

Esteemed Bac Ho, My father's really angry since he learned I was expelled from France because of the street protests. That's why I can't get work in the Civil Service, which is what *Cha* had planned. He's an old man and dependent on me. How were you able to balance such divided loyalties when you were my age? Can you, Uncle whom I have never met, forgive me for disobeying the Father who holds my hand and will not let go? The only way I can earn money now is by teaching French – the language of our oppressor – to the sons of Annamese merchants. (You wouldn't believe how difficult it is for them to master the future tense of *avoir*. They're so spoilt!) I long to join you in the jungle, but the Party says I'm more useful instructing workers with the Mass Literacy Campaign. Could you please write and make them change their mind? I dream of nothing but fighting in the hills and promise not to be a disappointment. *Your son in the cause, Trinh Anh Duy.*

Anh imagines being outcast in a fable

Immediately Ai Nam Ai Nu went looking for his father who was resting in the long grass. Plucking up his courage, the young deer explained how his friends had laughed, what did it mean. His father stood up, shaking his antlers menacingly and bellowed: *It means you are no son of mine. Ever since your mother died, I have lavished special care on you, and this is how you reward me for all my sacrifice? You are no son of mine.* The fawn hung his head and knew from that day forward, he must spend his life in the shadows.

Lucien sends his Mother a gift

Chère Maman, I hope you are pleased with the Annamese dress. The silk is so fine and the colours extraordinary. You will be the first woman in the Toulon region to possess such an exquisite gown. Send me a photograph when you wear it to the next charity event. As for my situation, it is too early to tell. Most in the Ministry seem to know the reason I have been sent here, though they are too polite to say so openly. It is all a matter of stares and whispers. That, with the heat and the endless crowds in every street, well I must admit to being often overwhelmed. Most disorienting of all, the poverty. No amount of reading prepares one. I began by giving money to every mother with a sickly child, but after several days I had to stop. There were simply too many. *Maman,* you may be moved by visiting the poor in our village but believe me, they are better off than the destitute here. I will write more soon. In the meantime, you know how much your eldest son thinks of you, even though he may sometimes let you down. *Ton fils, Lucien.*

The Housekeeper and Lucien (I)

While going over the accounts, Monsieur began talking about his private life. I didn't know what to do. He'd been drinking at lunch, said he's lonely *out here in the colonies* and needs to talk to someone. But we can't be friends. He's my Master, just feeling sorry for himself. How can I give advice to a man like him? Although I've worked twenty years for the French, I'll never be anything but a *coolie* in his eyes. Isn't he using me because he hasn't got any one of his own kind for comfort? But I have to admit, all this business with his mother is strange. He misses her more than a man his age should. Not healthy, almost as if he's still a child somehow. See, he's softened me up already. Playing on the fact I'm a mother myself. But I only have his side of the story, that she is *an unnaturally cold woman*. He's not going to fool me that easily.

Lucien searches for the provenance of his carving

One of the staff claims he spotted something similar here, in the store room of our Ethnological Museum. Entering the darkness, it becomes a cave of mystery, filled with the detritus of several expeditions up the Mekong. Spears and arrows peer through masks and feathers. Shelves buckle beneath the weight of notebooks and specimen jars – some with snakes and scorpions floating serenely in formaldehyde, others holding herbs and fungi. Tents, ropes and mosquito nets are draped over the jumble of anthropological finds, all awaiting a classification which may never be completed. Lanterns are piled atop maps, compasses and surveying equipment, the kerosene already dissolving their precious records. No carvings as far as I can see, but under these machetes, something that looks like bones.

Anh is confronted by a stranger at the Opera

I know I shouldn't like it anymore. I'm supposed to detest their culture, but for some reason, the music won't let me go. Once the audience enters, the guards allow us *coolies* to ascend the steps and look at the posters. A few of these artists I saw in Paris, but have no hope of buying a ticket now on my miserable wage. Sometimes I manage to hear a few notes from behind the doors. During interval, we're ordered back across the street, from where I gaze at the élite of Indochina, putting on a brave front even though they know the struggle for independence has well and truly begun. The women's jewellery sparkles like semaphore. The men lounge in dress uniforms which have never seen combat. Now one of them withdraws from the crowd and is heading this way. Is he about to call a guard and have me removed? His eyes lock onto mine, as though some kind of secret is shared.

Lucien is puzzled by a young man at the Opera House

Thank God for interval. I rush to the bar and knock back a brandy. With another in hand, I am ready for some fresh air and a look at what my colleagues call *la façade sérène* of this grand building. Well, I suppose it is an impressive imitation of the *L'Opera national de Paris*, though these columns do look slightly absurd, trumpeting their Corinthian filigree into the tropic night. No one told me how many boulevards radiate from these steps. Another example of our clever urban planning, designed no doubt by some of the men here, shouldering the burden of their military decorations. Now who is that in the shadows? What is this young *indigène* doing? I do not think they are allowed on the steps. I could have sworn he was staring at me. He is trying to hide behind one of the columns, but turns to take another look. Should I call a guard and have him removed? But there is something familiar about his face...

Anh tries to evade the French civil servant

This means trouble for sure – better run. But he shouts so pitifully I stop and turn. He's drunk and out of breath, wanting to know why I hang around the Opera. When I explain how I was a student and found a way of sneaking backstage in Paris, he laughs and praises my accent. He's just joking, surely? Then he offers to buy my ticket for the next performance. What an insult! This imperialist can't use me as his plaything. Still he follows, almost begging me now to teach him the history of Annam. Bac Ho says have nothing to do with the enemy, but there's a desperation in his voice which unbalances me, so I brush him off by saying we might meet one day in the Central Library. With that, he loosens his grasp and lets me go.

Lucien's statue slips through his fingers

He is that carving I have been carrying for years! I cannot let him go, cry out *Stop!* He looks puzzled but stands his ground. Explaining how he misses the Opera, I hope I do not make a fool of myself by offering to buy his ticket for the next performance. Wrong move. He is offended and swings to leave, so I blurt out something about local history. Perhaps he might teach me? My ploy works! I cannot let this fantasy slip through my fingers, now it has unexpectedly come to life. He mutters how he goes most afternoons to the Central Library and we could meet there. With that, my statue turns his face and is absorbed into the night.

The Housekeeper and Lucien (II)

I don't believe it. The Master says he's in love with a man. Even more of a shock, an Annamese man! He did show me that statue, saying it had the most beautiful face in the world. Guess he was trying to introduce the topic but I didn't pay attention because he was drunk, as usual. Any way the only *Ai Nam Ai Nu* I've ever known were so effeminate, you could spot them a mile off. Thought they must all be like that, but Monsieur Lucien doesn't show any signs. Wonder if the student acts like a woman? They were supposed to meet at the Central Library but after two days, he hasn't shown up. The Master's worked himself into such a state, he's practically begging me to help find the boy. I don't want to get involved but I'm such a softie. Not sure if Monsieur actually likes me, or if he's just using me because there's no one else. There's no denying he is unusually kind to all of us *domestiques,* not me only. Sort of asking us to do things, rather than ordering. I wonder if that explains it – being soft and gentle, I mean. If that's what makes him fall in love with men?

Lucien's rendezvous with Anh in the Central Library

Finally, after waiting in the main reading room every afternoon for three days, he shows up – looking even more nervous than I. Of course, I must initiate all the small talk to keep the conversation going. He wants to know about my work and is horrified when I mention the French Administration. It is all I can do to stop him bolting for the exit. Suggesting a walk, he retorts how it is unwise to be seen with a *coolie* like him. That the authorities do not approve of such associations. I reply, if there is no written prohibition, I am delighted to promenade with such a handsome young man. It is only then I witness my first Oriental blush.

Lucien nervously ventures a kiss

What a pleasure, our first restaurant meal. But being anywhere with you is truly a delight. There, I have made you blush again. You feel something also? You know what I mean – have you ever loved a man? Well, that is a good sign, not instantly withdrawing your arm. His name was Heng Tu? How alien that sounds compared to Lucien. This must be so confusing for you: I am French and older, but I trust there is still some hope? Ah, you let me stroke your hair. How strange to the touch. Not at all what I imagined from my carving. I agree, all this rather breaks the rules, does it not? Can I kiss you? Just on the cheek for now.

And Anh in great confusion allows himself to be kissed

Don't know what you mean about 'feeling the same'. No, I don't! Well (shouldn't be telling you this), there was a friend once. But that was years ago and he was Annamese like me. He was a poor student from the country who used to take lessons with my father. Then we trained together in martial arts. That's how it started. Nothing like this – you're French, the enemy! Don't know what to feel, the whole thing's wrong. But it's kind of exciting, holding your hand. This shouldn't be happening. Goes against everything I believe in. Shouldn't put my face so close to yours. No. Yes. You can kiss me.

Anh tells Lucien how Heng Tu changed his life

I used to watch Heng every afternoon, exercising in our garden, after his class with *Cha*. Splaying his arms like a bird, he whirled and dove. His hands became fists cracking the air in every direction, returning to stillness before venturing upon the next wave. Transfixed by this display, I ached to caress his body – incomparably better than my own puny machine. His muscles shone through beads of sweat. Spools of energy rippled from the breast bone along his arm, to explode at the fingertips. Each kick began in the stomach, unknotting itself along his legs to burst as electricity from the foot, smashing an invisible enemy's jaw. As the weeks passed, I sensed he was gaining strength from my gaze. He could feel the adoration streaming from my eyes, flowing through his chest and groin. He never called me *Ai Nam Ai Nu*. Not even as a joke. Instead when he was worn out, he would ask me to massage the pain from each limb. This was his ruse to unlock my power. He realised I would do anything to touch him. Inviting me to soothe a fatigued champion was how he tricked me into becoming an athlete myself. He unleashed a force I could never have imagined. Massage complete, I too was in a lather, so we poured water over each other's glistening skin. I would long for this moment all day.

Anh complains that Heng and the Party do not care

Heng was my hero – shining and strong. I adored him long before he transformed my body into the powerful weapon it is today. I'd do anything he wanted, even when it hurt. But once Father caught us together and said Heng was forbidden to enter our house again. Later I heard he started going with a girl! After all my worship and service. As if that wasn't bad enough, the Party doesn't value me either. What humiliation, teaching factory workers how to read and write! They sneer whenever I request military duty. Just because I'm a bit short for my age, a bit skinny. They've never got me to strip off and show what I can do. Then they'd see what a great soldier I'd be. And Bac Ho doesn't answer any of my letters, even though I offer to die for him every time I write.

But is surprised by how much Lucien does

He's the enemy. I should want to kill him, not feel like *this*. But Lucien is only too aware of my presence. He trembles just touching my shoulder. I know all about that carving he's cherished for years. It's strange, my own face in stone staring back. That's why he dreamt of coming here. As if he already loved me before we met. Who wouldn't hate the French, after what he's been through? Thrown into prison and exiled. And for something of no consequence like that night. He's all alone because they've made him an outcast. People stop talking and stare when he enters a restaurant. I know what that feels like – back in Paris, and here among the communist cadres. Pretty much my whole life. Maybe I could persuade him to do something for our movement. Get him to prove he really does love me. Ask him to hand over information, which I could pass on to the Party. They'd have to let me be a soldier then!

Anh's revelation to Ho Chi Minh about an undesirable friend

Esteemed Bac Ho, I'm afraid you might be angry with my news. Remember all the trouble I had with my father? Well, I've just met a new friend who makes me feel proud, after years of being told by *Cha* that I'm an embarrassment and failure. I'm sure you'd be pleased if it weren't for one fact – don't know how to say it – he's French. Before tearing this up, I beg you to listen. Although he works for the colonial administration, he supports our independence struggle. Isn't this something the Party could make use of? I'm sure I can find ways to persuade him to pass on vital documents which will help our cadres. See how we could turn my new contact to our advantage? There is more I wish to say about Lucien, but will wait for your blessing. *Your son in the cause, Trinh Anh Duy.*

The Bedroom the first morning

The maid enters without knocking as Monsieur Lucien had instructed, only to find a stranger in her master's bed. Anh is jolted out of sleep and tries to stand up forgetting he is naked, wrapping himself too late in the sheet. Both are frozen, not knowing what to do. Then almost at the same moment, they laugh.

The Housekeeper and Anh (I)

What a mess that young man is! He does annoy me, always going on about his freedom fighters. Young people get caught up in the strangest fantasies. Then the complete opposite: he's infatuated with all things French. As if his own country isn't good enough. Seems a betrayal to me, but he'd just joke that I'm too old to understand! He certainly enjoys the perks of living here in the Residence, though he'd never admit it. I've seen how he prances around in those new clothes the Master ordered. Don't blame him. Anyone would do the same, given half the chance. But then I think how much my own children had to suffer and I'm angry. Why doesn't Monsieur buy something for me, seeing how I have to comfort him almost every day? Then all the food Anh's allowed to give his family. His father says he's outraged the boy lives here, though it's never stopped him accepting a single scrap! Things were much simpler before I had Anh hanging around downstairs – with all his day dreams and puppy love.

Lucien's drunken thoughts tumble through the night

nothing but fleeting sex until now
all that danger
all that secrecy
never spent the night with anyone
wake up what a revelation
first time share more than lust
first time the other yearns for me
thirty-seven year old like a child
growth arrested
growth suppressed
no wonder wild-eyed
no wonder overwhelmed
coming from what depths
what power unleashed
pinch myself
make up for lost time

Anh takes Lucien to a local Buddhist temple

I need to catch my breath on the stairway. Anh jokes *such is the punishment for smoking.* Monks precede us, seeming to float, their feet never quite touching the steps. I marvel at the bronze carvings and all the pillars with their gilded quotations. Anh scorns me for being *hoodwinked by feudal parasites,* boasting such anachronisms will soon be swept away. But his Marxist tirade falls silent as we enter the courtyard and watch the monks, now motionless before their midday meal, staring straight ahead. Unobrustively, a novice slips into the centre and with the striking of a bell, takes a deep breath. Only a child, he begins to chant, his soprano solo slicing the air, revealing a vortex which evaporates before it can be apprehended. Then the monks are eating as if nothing out of the ordinary has occurred. Despite himself, Anh also is absorbed by the trance. Shaking him I whisper, *You felt it too, didn't you? How would Bac Ho account for that?*

The Housekeeper and Anh (II)

Seems he's always under my feet, with some new problem to talk about. Because I have sons of my own, he thinks I'm some kind of expert. Poor pet, his mother died so long ago, he's kind of latched on to me. Despite flaunting his high class French mannerisms, he really needs to be with his own people. Such lurid details about him and Monsieur, I have to make him stop. They both confide in me, but make me swear not to let the other know. How long before I snap, being pulled between these two? I try to reassure the young one, saying the Master's better than any of the French I've ever worked for. That's the truth, if nothing else is. *Take one day at a time,* I soothe this troubled boy. *Let's see what happens.*

Lucien writes to his mother of dresses and death

Chère Maman, I am disappointed you have not worn the Annamese dress. You agree the material and design are exceptional, yet you declare it to be *unsuitable for public display.* Years ago, you never worried about what people thought. Is it because of my arrest that you will not venture back into social circles? As for life here, you would be horrified to learn of the deaths caused by French plantation owners beating their native workers. In the few cases which are taken to court, culprits are either acquitted or instructed to pay the victim's family nothing but paltry damages. I know you to be a kind woman and, especially in the years since Papa's death, we have shared a great deal. Before what you refer to as 'my scandal', it seemed you had accepted me for the person I am. That is why I must tell you what is happening here in the name of France. You know only too well how much I need your support to stay sane in the cauldron Indochina has become. *Ton fils, Lucien.*

Vichy France joins forces with the Japanese

Hanoi Herald, 23 September 1940: *A diplomatic accord between the French Government and the Japanese Government has provided that Japan formally recognises the territorial integrity of Indochina and French sovereignty over all parts of the Indochinese Union. For their part, and in a spirit of friendship, all military facilities in Indochina will be conceded to the Japanese Army. This agreement is based on good faith and mutual esteem. Aware that he has fulfilled his duty, the Chef de la Colonie expects all citizens to accept this new situation without any reservation. More than ever before, French and Indochinese must gather around their leaders in a spirit of unanimity, work and love of the Fatherland.*

Lucien reluctantly participates in the Hanoi Trade Fair

Fewer delegates than the last one. They claim petrol rationing is responsible for the low turnout. Yet the etiquette is scrupulously observed, as if nothing has changed. The President of our Chamber of Commerce stands next to Indochina's Governor General in the front row. But the real power brokers of this charade are to be found in the row behind: Japan's Ambassador Extraordinary and the Chief of Tokyo's Economic Mission, almost giving the game away that it is they who pull the strings. I am surprised they do not insist on raising their own flag and playing the imperial anthem after *La Marseillaise*. In every other respect they treat us as if we were the Rising Sun's newest colony. We submit to their hand-shaking and smiles, grateful the make-believe has gone off without a hitch.

Pétain shakes hands with Hitler

Hanoi Herald, 24 October 1940: *This morning at Montoire-sur-le-Loire, His Excellency Marshal Pétain met Chancellor Hitler. The encounter proceeded with the utmost courtesy. Marshal Pétain was received with all the honours due to his rank. This meeting between the two Heads of State took place in order to discuss the current situation, in particular the means by which peace is to be restored in Europe. Both leaders agreed in principle to a policy of collaboration, the details of which will be discussed at a later date.*

Lucien defies Pétain's banner at the Opera House

Sacrilege, draping the image of Marshal Pétain over the place where Anh and I met. France's Nazi collaborator, pretending to be a benevolent grandfather with his Vichy motto – *Travail, Famille, Patrie*. Must our nation parade its cowardice before the whole world? The government has already allowed the Japanese access to all our military facilities in Indochina, and now this! I should stir myself from the stupor of apathy. If I continue working for such an administration, does it not amount to becoming a fascist myself? Despicable banner of Pétain, I curse you here on the Opera steps, and care not who hears my words.

Lucien gazes upon Anh while he sleeps

You are the closest to perfection I can imagine. That is why I light the candle and stare, hoping not to wake you. Nothing must spoil this moment. Nothing must change. Remain as you are now – eternal, save for the rising and falling of your breath. Each murmur proving you are real, that you are more than the carved creature I have treasured for years. Because of the heat, you toss away the sheets and stretch out, affirming your wonder to the world. Emboldened to stroke your thigh, I practise how to do so without disturbing you. This is my secret, my worship, transformed by each caress.

While listening to Lucien Anh worries through the night

Sometimes seems as though he might stop breathing. Sounds so far away. Maybe it's because of the cigarettes. I keep telling him he's got to cut down, but he just laughs it off. I count the seconds, waiting for his next breath. One. Two. Three. Other times he's so loud, a kind of groaning. Means he's having a bad dream. If I roll him on the side, that helps. Quiet for a while. Then he curls up and looks almost like a child, which is curious, considering he's older than me.

Lucien cleverly resolves a minor conflict

We are arguing about opera again. Anh claims *La Traviata* is greater than *Carmen* because of its pathos. How annoyed he is when I reply that is no surprise, as the Annamese are easily duped by sentimentality. This results in a pillow being aimed at my head, which I only narrowly avoid. Changing the subject, I ask for one of his folk tales. He can always recite another learnt in childhood, from what appears to be an endless store. So, peace returns.

Anh's Father in the Kitchen

They are preparing dinner when an old man in traditional clothes enters and stands at the door. No one pays him any attention so he clears his throat as he would to quieten a classroom: 'I am the father of Trinh Anh Duy. You are all Annamese. Why does no one put a stop to the shame my son commits in this house of our nation's oppressor?'

Lucien's drunken thoughts tumble further through the night

more years
more status
more cynic than Anh
but my joys
my fears
my disbelief
all fragile as his
unprepared for elation
unprepared for collapse
consumed by fire
can it still be me
why not give up the drink
this love
intoxication enough

The Housekeeper and Anh (III)

Anh is beside himself. So am I. Can't understand why the Master's started again, he hasn't touched a drop for weeks. Nothing like the drunks back in my village. How am I supposed to know what to do with a man like him, abnormal in every way? Hasn't gone to work at the Ministry two days in a row. He'll get into trouble. Nobody wants Government people snooping around, asking questions. We could lose our jobs if they find out what's been going on here. Monsieur keeps ranting on about someone called Pétain and how he's betrayed France. The only thing which makes him stop is when that strange boy threatens to leave. Monsieur puts the bottle down straight away. But Anh is barely a man himself, how's he supposed to keep control over someone like the Master? It's not fair. They both expect me to be on call night and day, to come running whenever they're in trouble.

In the morning Lucien is resurrected by Anh

Let me stay in bed. They will not miss me at the Ministry for a few hours more. There you go again, scolding that I drink too much. It does not suit you, sounding like *Maman*. I know only too well how strong you are, how deceptive your compact Asian physique. Let me gaze on your face a little longer, those incomparable lips. Then I will proceed to my duties. I promise. Yes, yes, we French are all liars, as you never tire of telling me. Now you can knock me out of bed. Use those martial arts of which you are so proud. Why not complete the job and throw water over this ruined head of mine? My revolutionary saviour, yet another miracle! You have enabled French diplomacy to rise and encounter the world.

Anh investigates the map of Lucien's body

You sag in places where I'm firm. Your body's a garment, worn and frayed, but somehow still holding together. There must be lots of secrets hidden in the folds of your skin. My finger glides along a vein from the wrist to where it disappears in the shoulder. Look, now I trace all the way to its destination – your heart. The pulse, just a tiny pump. Your body's a foreign world, nothing like my own. Because you welcome the stranger's entrance, my student hands can't wait to explore. I want this body of yours to become my home.

Anh takes Lucien to visit his mother's grave

There it is, at the end of the row. I was only eight when she died, she couldn't get out of bed for the last two years. Most of my memories are about how sick she was. Being the eldest, she expected me to do the housework and look after my brothers. I kept telling her she'd be well again, but when she grew worse, it only made her lose trust in me. Sorry, I shouldn't be bothering you with any of this. *Cha* never comes. He blames her for me turning out the way I have. That's what he says anyway. You're the only person I've brought here. Just wanted you to see. When she died, I couldn't breathe, couldn't hear anything for days. Seemed like another planet. No one on it except me.

Anh imagines another fable to fathom his dilemma

Once upon a time in the Land of Trinh, there were urchin boys who lived wretchedly, begging in the streets. One of their few pleasures were those days warm enough to swim in the local canal. Ai Nam Ai Nu was the only vagabond who did not participate on these rare occasions, because when he gazed at the others throwing off their rags and splashing about, a strange event occurred in his body. He dreaded if they ever discovered what it was, he would not be allowed to join them any more as they huddled in the laneways at night, trying to keep each other safe and warm.

Hoan Kien Lake, Hanoi

On Sundays, local families parade here and in the surrounding gardens wearing their best traditional clothes. Although Anh suggested several times that they should come, Lucien procrastinated, fearing they would attract too much attention, perhaps even be ostracised. But as Anh predicted, everyone smiles at them. A few men approach Anh with polite questions, Lucien knowing enough of the language now to recognise the words for *teacher* and *student*. This is the explanation they had prepared: that each is teaching the other his native language. Not only does no one appear to doubt their story, it simply elicits more smiles and deeper bows. Lucien begins to relax until he notices a Frenchman behind the trees.

Lucien savours Anh's scent fresh from the bath

Unsullied, as if the air itself were cleansed. From the bath, straight to sleep, the day's weariness evaporates in a flash. Freshness enfolds your limbs in its cocoon. Youth's fragrance cannot be borrowed, cannot be copied. Nor can it endure, as I sweep my net, hoping to catch its essence.

Spotted in the Restaurant

This Annamese restaurant is one of the few places where it is safe enough to be seen in public. They have been coming here for months without incident, but tonight one of Lucien's work colleagues enters accompanied by a local woman dressed provocatively in European clothes. Everyone stares as the waiter finds them a table. Lucien knows he must go over and greet this officer, but not before he can come up with an explanation for Anh's presence. The damage is done however, and more rumours are sure to fly around the Ministry.

Anh teaches the factory workers how to read

Gets better each time I'm here. Can see improvement in most of them, even after a month. Some reckon they're passing on my ideas to family at home. No one's ever said anything about me being short or skinny either. Quite the opposite, they treat me with respect. Kind of embarrassing. Never thought this is what I'd end up doing with all my years of study, but guess it does help the revolution. Think I begin to see that now. What's happening over there? They're calling me to eat with them. Say they've brought special food for their teacher. Me.

Anh composes slogans with the workers

Don't know whose idea it was, but now everyone's involved. Some are getting pretty fired up, making this poster: Tham gia với những người nông dân để tiêu diệt các tiếng Pháp (Join with the peasants to destroy the French). Then I suggest: Công nhân công nghiệp là anh em của bạn (Factory workers are your brothers), which makes them laugh a lot. But this is the one I'm proudest of: Học đọc là một vũ khí chống lại kẻ thù (Learning to read is a weapon against the enemy). Because that makes me feel like a soldier after all.

Lucien's drunken thoughts collapse into the night

Indochina exile
colleagues say the natives not human
unworthy of love
so they think I'm mad
or traitor
always on guard
shield true nature
shame guilt
enemy among my own people
masquerade for their drama
Maman
her silence accusation
can't breathe

Lucien grows into a new idea of himself

Chère Maman, you know I was ashamed when Gabriel submitted to the Nazi occupation. But that he should work with the Vichy police, what a disgrace! I dream of having the courage to join the very forces my brother now rounds up for *Les Boches.* I have been silent for too long. Inebriation, a coward's response, while my lover Anh endangers himself more than I have in a lifetime. As if I were not already chastised by this young man's bravery, now I have another reason to enter the fray: to prove I could become a better man than my brother, the collaborator. Dare I hope, for the first time in my life, I may have some integrity? That I am capable of redemption, even in your eyes? As though until now I was wearing the wrong body. Shedding my former skin, I breathe more easily. I am discovering conviction makes for less guilt than being a swillpot. *Ton fils, Lucien.*

The Housekeeper and Lucien (III)

The Master's taking a huge risk giving that list to Anh, knowing it will go straight to the Viet Minh. Says it's to make up for what his brother's doing back in France. But I know that's not the reason. It's because he's obsessed by that boy and lost all touch with reality. Monsieur imagines Anh is *a hero*, so he wants to prove he can be brave also. Sacrificing everything for love! Or what he calls *love*. How can such an educated, such a privileged man throw his life away? People like me would never risk our lives for something so extravagant. We know food and a roof over your head count for more than anything else, when all's said and done.

Anh brings Lucien to help with his student workers

Well, they seem to accept him OK. Some stares and whispers, but that's all. He broke the ice by trying out a few Annamese phrases with such a bad accent, it set them all laughing, so he hammed it up some more and had them in stitches. Then a couple of the bolder ones ventured what little French they know and he began demonstrating how to improve their pronunciation. I continue with the others, making posters which we'll put up in the old town later tonight. After five minutes, just for fun, I call out to those gathered round him: *Get that white man to come over here and help us. We coolies have been running after them long enough. Now it's their turn to sweat and do some real work!* This created pandemonium of course, especially as Lucien didn't know what I'd said. But giggling all the way, they lead him over here and put a paint brush in his hand, which he cheerfully accepts.

Lucien cooks for *Les Domestiques*

He'd been promising for weeks but only now is he at the stove, with Anh helping of course, since it is local food he's offered to prepare. He tried to keep the servants out of the kitchen but they are stubbornly curious and he gives up. They are all joking around the table, giving contradictory instructions. Everyone is so relieved to see the Master sober and happy, they could have no idea that this was to be their last shared meal.

Lucien copies the blacklist for Anh

There is no turning back now. Once this is handed over, I am working for my country's enemy. After all this time wallowing on the sidelines, even a wretch like me must finally step on stage. Some of Anh's comrades are named here. They need to know who is being watched, who remains undetected. Compared to the danger they face, my role barely counts. Anh thinks I am a hero, but his vision is clouded by youth.

Anh imagines a prince who will save his life

Many years ago, during the reign of King Tran Thuan Ton, there was a group of guttersnipes who survived on food scraps discarded by the palace kitchen. One evening, the cook demanded they sing for their supper. Try as they might, the urchins' efforts were all cut short, their voices dismissed as worse than the wailing of cats. Soon one of the courtiers appeared, demanding to know the cause of this frightful noise. As Ai Nam Ai Nu was the next in line, the Mandarin challenged him to do better than the others. Taking a deep breath, the waif began a folk song, his voice growing in beauty as the tale unfolded. While the final notes ebbed away, the silence was broken by the courtier: *Have this brat washed, clothed and brought before the Prince. Perhaps the court will find such talent in an urchin amusing.* As the boy followed down the corridor, the Mandarin whispered to him: *If you can truly entertain His Highness, your life will change more than you could imagine.*

Anh is about to deliver the blacklist to his comrades

Let's see what the Party thinks of me now! They're suspicious I have a French friend sympathetic to our cause, but don't want to ask too many questions. They're waiting to see how useful the information is. But what if they expect me to do this on a regular basis? I'd have to worm out of it somehow, say it's becoming too dangerous. Didn't worry about that before. Only how it'd benefit me, not what it might mean for Lucien. Wouldn't get any sympathy from the comrades if he was arrested, that's for sure. Couldn't imagine anything coming between me and the Party. But now, I can't bear the thought of Lucien being dragged off to prison. Haven't felt like a misfit since I've been with him. Used to joke that he made me *flourish as a plant in the sun*. How would I survive without him?

Fragments of Propaganda from Uncle Ho in the jungle

After the rain, fine weather. With the blink of an eye, the universe throws off its muddy clothes. Be mindful, the tempest is a chance for the cypress tree to show its strength and stability. If the tiger holds his ground to fight, the elephant will crush him with his weight. But if he stays agile and keeps his mobility, he will finally vanquish the elephant, who will bleed to death from a thousand cuts. This is what the French will write in letters to their mothers: *death waits for us in every pothole, every bush, every pond*. Meanwhile, our guerrilla soldier swims through the people like a fish swims through the sea. When the prison doors are open, only then will the real dragon take flight. Write in such a way that you can be understood by both young and old, even the children. In the past, poets would sing of nature's charms: hills, streams, moon and wind. But now a poem must have steel. Today, the poet must learn to wage war.

Lucien pleads with his mother to break silence

Chère Maman, I need you to love me, or say you do. Or, that you know I am a good man – or at the very least, you believe I could become one. But all I hear is silence. Although Gabriel has not caused the 'scandal' I did, now that he works with the Vichy police, surely you cannot support him? Perhaps you will never grow fond of Anh himself, but you must approve of the effect he has on me: these days, I barely drink at all. Sometimes, I accompany him when he teaches in the factories. Can you imagine me, having wallowed in self-hatred for years, now reaching out to help others? Joining a movement that will transform the lives of thousands? I cannot bear him to see me as I was before. Even if it is nothing but the vanity of a middle-aged man in the presence of this trained athlete, I am motivated to be better. To be full of purpose, perhaps ultimately, a person of whom you could be proud. *Ton fils, Lucien.*

A living statue receives Lucien's nocturnal kiss

It is in between breaths, when completely still, that you become the carving itself. Even now, I cannot believe you lie here in my bed. Each night, holding the candle, I know you will not wake beneath my gaze. But this is the first time, positioned precisely, I dare to kiss you while asleep. There, I embrace your lips so they impress themselves on mine. Like a stamp, a perfect copy. Even after I lift away, the imprint remains.

The Housekeeper and Lucien (IV)

He's putting us in danger, me and the staff. As soon as the security police learn what Monsieur's done, they'll want to question all of us. How much did we know? Did we help him? Even if we get through the interrogation without being beaten up, they'll probably dismiss us anyway. I'm too old to find a position in a new residence. I'll have to go back to the provinces and live with one of my children and his family, who barely have enough to eat as it is. And all for what? For some foreigner's stupid obsession?

Lucien's early morning arrest at the Residence

That is the police, banging on the front door. I was right to tell Anh to stop coming here. Ever since copying the blacklist, I felt I was being observed. Anh wondered if I was melodramatic, arranging for the Housekeeper to place a signal at the gate in the back lane. But he will be grateful when he checks and knows he must leave Hanoi immediately. It depends how much they rough me up, but I cannot be sure what information I may reveal. Now they are on the stairs. Only seconds before they break into my room. This is the real test, is it not? I have often imagined this moment, even picturing it is Gabriel and his Vichy police who have come to take me. My transformation is about to be put to the proof. How well will the drunkard perform his new role?

Anh in the back lane knows what it means

That's it: the gate left open with a sack of laundry. Lucien's been arrested! He was right to make those plans. Thank God I warned the Party there might be trouble. That if I don't turn up at nine each morning, it means I had to leave in a hurry. They'll know which comrades need to go into hiding. Suppose I should be happy. I get to be a soldier with Bac Ho at last. But right now, I'd much rather be with Lucien than those freedom fighters! What's worse, it's me who got him into trouble. He did it for my sake. Me and my dreams of being a bloody hero!

Lucien languishes in Hanoi's political prison

Maison Centrale's cells are dirtier and smaller than those in Toulon. And the colonial police here are much rougher than our Metropolitan *gendarmes*. My brother would not be able to get me out of this, even if he wanted to. Did Anh manage to escape in time? It would be strange if my arrest propels him to finally become the soldier of his dreams. I should not have read all those interrogation files. I know the torture techniques only too well. Which method will they employ on me, a traitor, no longer *one of their own?* Will it be days – or only hours – before I crack and endanger the revolution by signing anything they thrust beneath my broken nose?

The Housekeeper and Anh (IV)

How will I break the news to his father? Perhaps he might be pleased his son is now acting like a real man, not as the *Ai Nu Ai Nam* of before. That's the angle I'll use anyway. I'll also make him proud the boy has not abandoned his own country, even after all that time with Monsieur. Must admit, I do worry how he's coping in the jungle. Not the kind of life for a student like Anh. Won't be long before he's disillusioned with the whole thing. All that talk of fighting and independence – nothing but the daydreams of youth. Then I try not to think about how soft his hands were as he nestled on my shoulder, calling me *Mother*.

Anh's first glimpse of Uncle Ho at Viet Minh headquarters

In the jungle with my guerrilla comrades. Can't believe I'm finally here, after escaping the capital. Hope Lucien's been able to talk himself out of trouble by now. Saw Bac Ho once coming out of the bunker. Could hardly believe it was him, he looked so thin and tired. Shorter than I imagined too. A letdown after all these years. Maybe he's going to hand the leadership over to someone else? There were lots of comrades milling round. They burst out laughing when I tried to explain about my letters: *Reckon Bac Ho's got time to read stuff from a city slicker like you? Who do you think you are?*

Anh cannot sleep in the cave

Can't find the right position, the ground's too hard. All of us have to squeeze into this rocky space, only way to avoid being spotted by French planes. Smells awful. Not enough water to wash ourselves, let alone our clothes. Nearly all these fighters are peasants. They speak so rough, sometimes I can't understand. They laugh at my *posh accent*. Heard a few joking my skin's too soft to be a soldier, reckon I need to be toughened up. That's why they've got me on latrine duty more than anybody else in the whole unit. I'm last in line for food and ammo, though they snigger I could work my way up the queue, once I learn what to do with my *pretty face.*

Anh misses Lucien and mutters French in his sleep

Think of him a lot. (And how soft his bed is, compared to this stony floor). God, I had it good with Lucien. Even when he was drunk, he treated me with more respect than these peasants could possibly imagine. Like he understood me better than I did myself. Got to be careful, sometimes I blurt out stuff in French. The colonial language has almost become second nature. That makes them dislike me even more – they reckon I prefer hobnobbing with the enemy to being with my own people. Wonder if I say anything in my sleep. Curling up to Lucien for all that time, I might mumble his name. That'd make these hicks go crazy. They'd shoot me right on the spot.

Anh comes up with a shrewd new scheme

How stupid to think Bac Ho read any of my letters. His secretaries would've thrown them out with all the other hero-worshipping stuff sent to him. I was scribbling to a shadow, babbling to a blank wall! Got to come up with another plan. That was enemy communication I saw delivered a few minutes ago. Rumour is the French want safe passage for their wounded along one of the roads under Viet Minh control. If only I could get someone in HQ to see that I write faultless bureaucratic French. (Learnt a few tricks looking over Lucien's shoulder when he had to complete dispatches from the Residence). If I could be promoted by serving the revolution that way, mightn't get manhandled by these bloody oafs moaning for their girlfriends every night. I'm not strong enough to fight them all off, so may as well use my other weapon – cunning.

Lucien wraps the carving in his final letter

Anh, I hope you got away in time and that you are happy with Bac Ho and his freedom fighters. They must be pleased to have such a resourceful comrade. I saw how the factory workers came to admire you. No doubt the Viet Minh's fighting arm will feel the same. As for me: I did better than expected. Mostly because of you. When my interrogators realised I knew nothing about the Party's structure, they relented. You were right not to reveal any details. It saved me quite a few beatings. I feel some pride, that no one now can call me a useless drunk. Here are some verses written by Ho. My guards have been quoting them for weeks, so I know them by heart: *The morning sun shines over the prison wall/Driving away the shadows and miasma of hopelessness/A life-giving breeze blows across the earth /A hundred imprisoned faces smile once more.* Puzzling, is it not, a French prisoner quoting lines from the leader of our Viet Minh? That is one of the transformations brought about by knowing you. Here, I fold this letter around the carving I've carried for years – never daring to imagine it could become flesh. *Ton frère, Lucien*

The August General Uprising advances towards Hanoi

Revolutionary Flame (Viet Minh broadsheet), August 1945: *Comrades, we bring you glorious news of our Nationalist struggle. Now that the Japanese have surrendered along with the imperialist French, we are on the brink of independence. Bac Ho has ordered all Revolutionary Committees to raid the landlords' granaries and distribute rice freely to the people. Most villages and towns in the North have already embraced their Viet Minh liberators. It is only a matter of days before we seize control of Hanoi itself. Hesitate no longer. Join in the struggle to create our new nation!*

Unable to make contact Lucien ponders his execution

It will all be over in an hour. They are sharpening the blade outside the bars of my window. I have walked past the guillotine for weeks, almost forgetting its purpose. *Maman* may receive my letter in time. At least I can imagine her thinking of me. But I am not sure what I wrote to Anh will reach him. It is most unlikely he will ever learn of my fate. Perhaps I will beg one last drink before ascending the scaffold. I must not let them see me shake. They promise it will be a single cut. Quick and clean. Thus, even at my traitor's end, I may suffer less than my fellow prisoners, the local insurgents. Am I delirious, hoping my death could advance their cause in any way? Will Anh now believe I love him? Again, the blade.

Anh confronts Ho Chi Minh with Lucien's sacrifice

He's making the speech right now on the balcony of the Opera House, declaring independence for our new nation. I've snuck up the back stairs to challenge him when he finishes. He should remember our last meeting when I was still on the General Staff. He listened to my advice then. After agonising for months, not knowing what'd happened to Lucien, it's a cruel joke I should only learn the day when our Viet Minh troops liberate Hanoi. Should have been a moment of joy – as it was for my comrades. But for me, the worst day of my life. Still can't believe it, or say the words. Hope there's been some kind of mistake. What happened to Lucien. What happened – Bac Ho must be told that a Frenchman *was murdered* for refusing to give information, for protecting me. But I know he will never make any public acknowledgement. After all, he pretended not to understand our friendship when I tried to tell him years ago. Never mentioned it again, but now that I know the reason for Lucien's death, I'm ashamed of my silence. I'm determined to make him see the proof in my hands. The least I can do for the man who changed my life, stand before Bac Ho and declare: *Although Lucien was one of the hated French, he died for our country. Forgive me then for loving him.*

Anh reads Lucien's letter in the condemned man's cell

Lucky the guard didn't destroy this. He must think it contains information the Party could use. Ironic he gives it to me because of my uniform. He's never seen so many decorations as those lining my chest – all empty boasts. Our Propaganda Department meddling with the truth yet again. How typical of you, Lucien, to write as if you're a character of no importance. Reading these lines, no one'd ever know that you sacrificed yourself. Stepping into the cell, hope I can feel you here. But it's only the emptiness, your absence which embraces me. Can't breathe, as if you took all the air with you. The walls begin to shake. Nothing staying still. Lucien, why did I not – ?

Anh hopes to be healed

Returning two weeks later, I begin to recover. At least the cell walls aren't caving in today. Everything still in slow motion though. The panic's gradually dying down. If I close my eyes, close my eyes, let's try – yes, your hand is there. Trembling as it touches my shoulder, just like before. What was it you said in the letter? You want a custodian for the carving? Well, lucky you can't see me now. You wouldn't be pleased by how the years have hardened my skin. Look, there's even a scar on what you used to call *this perfect face.*